BASIC GUITAR ADJUSTMENTS & SETUPS

by John Boehnlein

ISBN 0-7935-7466-8

7777 W. BLUEMOUND RD. P.O BOX 13819 MILWAUKEE, WI 53213

Visit Hal Leonard Online at
www.halleonard.com

BASIC GUITAR ADJUSTMENTS & SETUPS

CONTENTS

FOREWORD

As popular as the guitar is today, playing the instrument does not come naturally to a beginning student. The ability to master any instrument is achieved only through continuous practice and repetition. The critical component (study and effort), can not be trivialized because one is not born with an inherent ability of instrumental mastery. As a consequence, the level of musical competency will grow in relation to the amount of effort one invests.

Along with the popularity of playing the guitar, there is a concurrent interest in how the guitar works. John's book directs itself to the basics of how a guitar should play and encourages players to repair and maintain their instrument so they will not become discouraged as they pursue their study of music. He has written a simple book of information valuable to many guitarists. The knowledge of how to maintain an instrument, and a grasp of its basic functions, are sound strengths to develop.

I trust you will find the information presented herein to be helpful in the maintenance of your instrument.

Kurt Wright
Wright Guitars
Cleveland, Ohio
December, 1996

PREFACE

The purpose of this book is to provide guitar and bass players basic guidelines for setting up and adjusting their own instruments. The text covers general procedures for setting action, pickups, intonation, necks, etc. In addition, long- and short-term maintenance also is discussed. The book is not intended as a reference source for extensive repairs, modifications, construction, design, or instrument building. Rather it serves as a "how to" guide for the do-it-yourselfer.

When I was a guitar student at Musicians Institute in Hollywood, California, I started a small business in my apartment called Wild Dutch's Guitar Hospital. I would do minor repairs, adjustments, and set-ups for students, teachers, and some of the local bands. Generally the work was run of the mill, no frills, and uncomplicated. Players would pay me good money to make their gear "right." I always thought if these players had a simple and straightforward source of information on how to fix their own instruments, they could have done the majority of the work themselves. People often asked me to instruct them in repair procedures, but unfortunately I never had the time. I was very busy as a student and running my own business. Hopefully, this basic guide will help those of you wanting to do your own work, and provide the information required to do that work.

Please be advised this book covers only simple, routine, maintenance procedures. Instruments which are damaged, broken, warped, cracked, or require extensive rehabilitation and reconstruction are beyond the scope of this book. Please refer these types of repair work to a qualified and experienced professional luthier familiar with advanced guitar repair.

Properly adjusted instruments will show dramatic improvements in tone, sustain, gain, playability, and tuning stability not to mention longevity. I have always been amazed, as have my clients, what a difference a set up can make, even on an inexpensive, stock instrument. The added "presence" and "aliveness" can be incredible. By simply making the instrument "right" and allowing it to function and "ring" as a complete system, audible and playable differences become apparent.

Fixing your guitar or bass can be a challenging, enjoyable, and rewarding experience. You get a sense of satisfaction and accomplishment from doing your own work. Everything I discuss in this book can be done by anyone with the ability to use simple hand tools. Most guitar and bass adjustments are quick, simple, and easy to understand. Even if you have never done any of your own adjustments before, I think you will find this book intriguing as you see how easy it is to work on your own instrument. Enjoy!

ABOUT THE AUTHOR

"Wild Dutch"

John Boehnlein is an internationally recognized expert in the field of guitar technology. He is the owner of Wild Dutch's Guitar Hospital in Independence, Ohio. In addition to *Basic Guitar Adjustments and Set-Ups for Beginners*, John also is the author of the *High Performance Marshall Handbook*. He is a graduate of Cleveland State University as well as the Musicians Institute Prelude Program. He has a wide variety of experience in nearly every facet of the music business.

ACKNOWLEDGEMENTS

Eternal thanks and gratitude to my folks, Frank and Mary for always supporting me no matter what my adventures, and Lord knows there have been plenty! Special thanks to Greg and Clyde at Timeless Guitars, all at Musician's Institute, Dale Titus, Kurt Wright, Brian Pentecost and John St. John, Beth Janicek, Jimmy Z, Joni Penington, Gary Davis, all at Hal Leonard Corporation, Jeannette Mishler, John Carruthers, Jerry Blaha, Jerry Rector, Kurt Carson, and Dan Kosak.

CHAPTER 1
TOOLS

V ery few tools are required to do the work you are about to undertake. Tools are a necessary part of the adjustment process, but fortunately, very few specialized tools are needed. Most of the tools you will need can be found around the house, at a neighborhood garage sale, or at the local hardware store. Common tools such as screwdrivers, sockets, and wrenches are usually easy to find. I have listed everything you will need and explain each item's use. Also included is a small list of supplies you will find helpful .

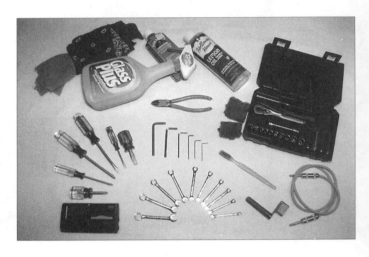

LIST OF TOOLS

1. **Screwdrivers:** Various sizes, both flathead and Phillips. A good portion of your work will be done with screwdrivers.

2. **Sockets:** A small one quarter inch drive set in either standard or deep-well American. Very few instruments, except some bass guitars, require anything larger than a one half inch socket. A one quarter inch drive set will meet the strength and torque requirements of your work. A ten millimeter and eleven millimeter socket in a deep-well size will also be necessary for tightening tuning post nuts and metric control hardware.

3. **Wrenches:** If you do not have a socket set, wrenches will suffice for most of your adjustments. However, wrenches will not reach every nut on every guitar. A small set of wrenches up to one half inch in size will handle most jobs.

4. **Allen Wrenches:** A modest assortment of American and metric sizes of allen wrenches are some of the few specialty tools required for bridge and truss rod adjustments.

5. **String Winder:** Not a true necessity, but a great time saver. A string winder allows for quick re-stringing instead of time consuming winding with the fingers.

6. **Workplace:** You'll need a large, flat space with a large blanket or piece of carpet to protect the surface and your guitar. Make sure your work place is not mom's antique dinning room table or new kitchen counter!

7. **Furniture cleaner and glass cleaner:** Takes off dirt, grime, gook, goo, and all other stuff that accumulates on your guitar.

8. **Lemon Oil:** A real necessity, it helps preserve open grain woods such as rosewood, ebony, or any unfinished wood.

9. **Electronic Guitar Tuner:** Not a tuning fork or pitch pipe! This is an absolute must for tuning the strings to proper pitch and setting intonation correctly.

10. **Synthetic Steel Wool:** Use this to clean fingerboards and remove scratches and oxidation from frets. It is very handy for smoothing minor fingerboard imperfections and making fingerboards appear almost brand new. *DO NOT USE ON LACQUERED WOOD!* Use only 000-extra fine grade, unless your fingerboard is extremely dirty. If this is the case, work from coarse steel wool down to fine.

11. **Cleaning Rags:** Clean soft rags for cleaning, buffing, and polishing.

12. **Toothbrushes:** Toothbrushes work great for cleaning cracks, crevices, and hard to reach places.

CHAPTER 2

INSTRUMENT INSPECTION AND FIRST STEPS

The first thing to do before beginning any repair on your instrument is to take a good look at its condition. Then ask yourself the following questions:

1. What kind of shape is it in?

2. Is anything loose or bent?

3. Does anything look abnormal or out of place?

4. Does it have noticeable sound or playability problems?

5. Has the instrument been modified from its original construction?

6. When was it last serviced?

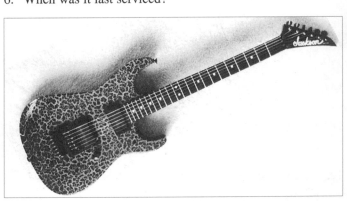

Overall photo of instrument to be repaired

Even the untrained eye will be able to make some type of evaluation from a visual inspection. The purpose of your initial inspection is to determine what the instrument is or is not doing. Both a visual and sonic (playing) examination will provide a relatively complete diagnosis of the instrument's condition, although some problems may not be uncovered until the instrument is in the process of adjustment. A thorough examination will give you a good idea of how much time as well as what type of work will be required to properly set up the piece.

Playing the guitar

Start by looking at how the instrument is currently set up. Look, play, and listen. After a few minutes of basic examination, you will have a good idea what kind of job lies ahead. After you have a general idea about the instrument, you are ready to start.

Begin by removing the strings. This should be done slowly, one string at a time, either by hand or with a string winder. Never cut or clip the strings to remove them quickly. This sudden unloading of string tension can cause massive stress changes to the neck of the guitar.

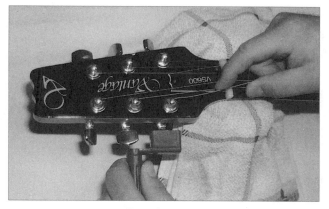

Unwinding strings

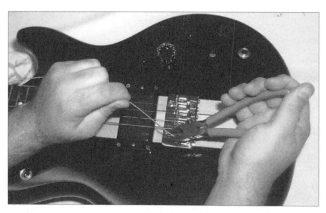

Clipping strings at bridge

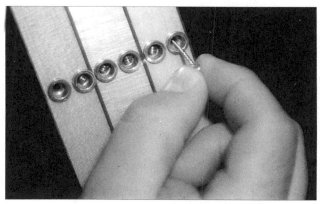

Removing strings from bridge

CHAPTER 3
TIGHTENING AND CLEANING

Once you have removed the strings from the instrument, you are ready to begin your setup. Your next task will be to tighten the various screws, nuts, and bolts on the instrument. These include neck screws, tuning machines, controls, etc. All hardware and fasteners should be tightened down just enough to prevent rattles and buzzes except for the neck plate bolts which should be extremely tight.

Tightening tuning machines

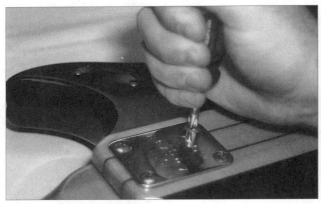

Tightening neck screws

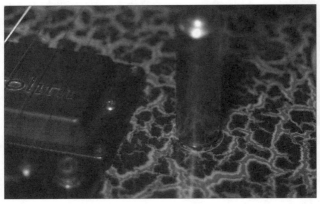

Tightening controls

Next it is time to clean your guitar. This will help maintain the finish, keep moving parts moving, maintain the instrument's value, and contribute to a clearer tone. For general instrument cleaning, glass cleaner and a small soft rag will suffice on metal, plastic, and wood surfaces that are finished. For older instruments with a large amount of of buildup, some furniture cleaner and elbow grease will usually do the trick.

Cleaning the finish

Fingerboards—especially open, unfinished grains like ebony and rosewood—are notorious for being dirty and usually require a bit of effort. Here is where you want to use synthetic steel wool and some furniture cleaner. Simply scrub, with the grain, along the length of the fretboard. Apply firm, even pressure across the fingerboard. This combination of an abrasive pad and furniture cleaner lifts dirt and helps work some oil into the grain. Once you are done scrubbing, take a clean rag and wipe off the mess. Use a toothbrush to get underneath the fret wire to finish the cleaning. A light application of lemon oil, rubbed into the grain and left to dry, will keep the finger board from drying or cracking by preserving the moisture content of the wood.

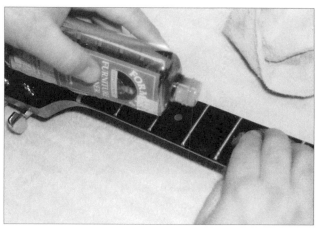

Cleaning the fingerboard

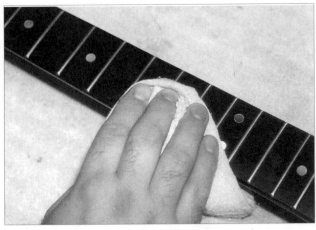

Wiping the fingerboard

Oiling the fingerboard

For optimum cleaning, remove hardware such as knobs, bridges, and tailpieces that may be caked with dirt. Some scrubbing with a toothbrush and dish soap will clean these pieces in no time. Let them dry thoroughly before reinstallation.

Cleaning the hardware

CHAPTER 4

RE-STRINGING

In all my years of doing guitar maintenance, I cannot remember meeting a player who knew how to correctly put strings on their instrument! This sounds amazing, but it is true. Even more amazing, many players would still have on their instrument the same set of strings I had installed months before. Why? They were not sure how to put the strings back on correctly. Correct string installation is the foundation from which the entire setup is based. Proper re- stringing contributes markedly to tuning stability, sustain, intonation, and maintaining a balanced tone.

In this chapter, I will show you how to re-string your instrument so it has good sustain, stays in tune, intonates precisely, and has an even, balanced tone.

HOW TO PUT STRINGS ON:

1. *Carefully* remove one string at a time from the package. Slowly unwrap the string, allowing it to unfold naturally. Do not bend or kink the string as this will make it unusable. Be careful to keep the string away from your eyes or other soft body parts, as the ends are very sharp.

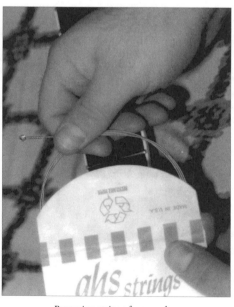

Removing strings from package

2. Insert the string into the bridge or tailpiece carefully. Again, do not bend, kink, or force the string into position. Insure that the ball end is firmly seated. (For Floyd Rose style tailpieces, the ball end and "wrap-around lock" of the string must be removed. Insert the cut-off end fully into the bridge saddle.)

Feeding string through bridge

3. Pull the string straight to the head-stock.

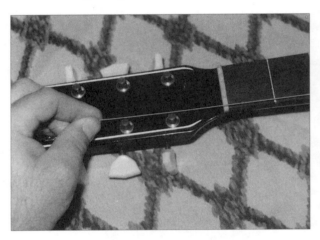

Pulling string to headstock

4. Insert the string into the hole in the post.

Inserting string into tuning post

5. Pull the string through, allowing enough slack to wind the string 3-10 times around the post.

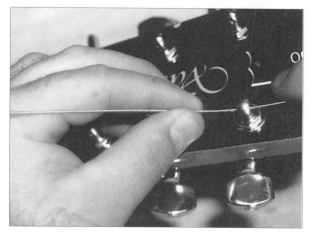

Adjusting string slack

6. Bring the string around the post and back under itself.

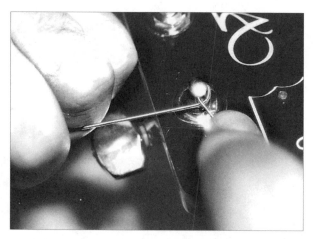

Bring string around post

7. Loop the string up, around, and over itself and pull it taut. This prevents slippage or movement around the post.

Loop string around

8. Begin winding the string around the post. Windings should be neat, even, and precisely wound from the top down. I recommend using most of the post for your windings.

When winding, be careful of the excess string as it has a tendency to whip around. Also, wind with one hand and feed the string to the post with the other hand. Keep tension on the string at all times. Do not allow the string to drag through the nut as this will quickly wear out the nut slots.

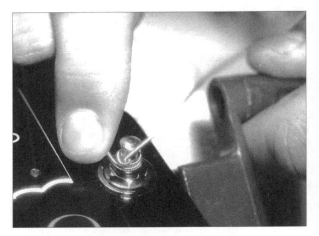

Winding string

9. Tune to pitch, stretch, and re-tune.

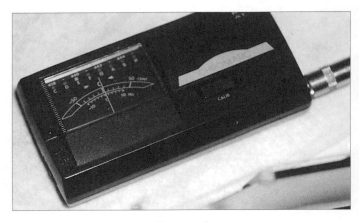

Tune to pitch

Stretch string

10. Insure that the strings are traveling in the most direct and straight path between the nut and the post. This prevents binding in the slots and provides proper downward pressure across the nut.

11. When you are done, clip the excess string as close as possible at the post. Any sharp edges left on the string should be pushed close to the post so as not to protrude.

Clip excess string

The completed winding

The completed restringing

CHAPTER 5

NECK ADJUSTMENTS

Neck adjustments are the most sensitive of all the procedures you will perform during your setup. Extreme care, gentleness, and patience must be taken. Neck adjustments are essential to proper playability, action, and intonation.

Most steel string electric and acoustic guitars and basses have the capacity to have their warp, or relief, changed from flat to convex or concave by means of a metal rod in the neck. This rod is called a *truss rod* and is used to change neck tension. Neck tension adjustments may need to be performed for a variety of reasons including humidity and climatic changes, shock from travel, string gauge changes, or fret wear compensation.

Once you have properly installed the strings on the instrument, they should be stretched several times to remove their natural slack. Tune to pitch and let the instrument settle for about ten or fifteen minutes. Tune up again and you are ready to make your adjustments to the neck.

Truss rod access is generally gained either at the head stock or at the heel of the neck. Adjustments are made with an Allen wrench, socket, or screwdriver depending on the particular brand of instrument.

Remove the truss rod cover

Begin by sighting down the neck from the headstock along the edge of the fingerboard. Is the neck bowed? or curved? If there is a hump in the neck, you will need to subtract tension. If there is a dip in the neck, you will need to add tension.

Generally speaking, the object of a truss rod adjustment is to balance the tension of the truss rod against the string tension. A very slight, barely perceptible relief in the neck is optimum. A neck with a back-bow (a hump) or twist is unusable if it can not be adjusted out.

To adjust the truss rod do the following:

1. Turn clockwise to add tension, turn counter clockwise to subtract tension.

2. Continually check tuning, as neck relief is tension dependent.

3. Go slowly, only one quarter of a turn at a time.

4. Apply smooth, even torque to the tool during adjustment.

5. Give the neck five or ten minutes to settle into the tension adjustments you have performed to the truss rod.

Truss rod adjustment

Once satisfied with the relief in the neck, you are ready to move on to adjusting the action.

CHAPTER 6

ACTION ADJUSTMENTS

After finishing the truss rod procedure, you must adjust the action for playability of the instrument. Depending upon the particular bridge type on your instrument (and there are many), there are different ways to make those adjustments. Action is extremely subjective and will have to be set to your particular playing style and taste.

Action can be defined as the distance a string must be depressed to reach the fret and sound a note. Instruments with extremely high action can be difficult to play and may present problems in terms of intonation and compensation at the bridge. Action that is too low can result in fret buzz and string choking. You will have to find that comfortable medium in between. Many players prefer their action as low as possible without buzz or string-choke. Choking is what happens when the string is bent across the fretboard and dies out or "chokes."

Action adjustments are accomplished by raising or lowering the strings in relation to the fretboard. Tune-O-Matic and Floyd Rose bridges have simple bass and treble side adjustment screws. Fender-style bridges will generally allow adjustment for either one or two strings at a time. (This includes bass guitars.) Individual string height adjustments—as opposed to whole bridge height adjustment—provide a more precise level of height adjustment. Most acoustic guitars and basses have nonadjustable action and will be treated separately later in this chapter.

TUNE-O-MATIC STYLE BRIDGES

The following procedure should be used to adjust the action on a Tune-O-Matic style bridge:

1. Screw tailpiece down until the high and low E strings are just above the back of the bridge to maximize string angle and sustain.

2. Re-tune guitar to pitch.

3. Raise or lower bass and treble sides of bridge by turning the adjustment screws or thumb wheels until the open strings ring clearly with no buzz when plucked.

4. Adjust the bass and treble sides in small increments until all notes can be fretted or bent with no buzz or choke.

5. Remember all adjustments must be performed with the strings at pitch. Consequently you must re-tune the strings and recheck your work several times as you are fine-tuning the action adjustments.

6. You must continue to perform incremental action adjustments and string re-tuning until a satisfactory balance between the bass and treble sides has been achieved across the fretboard.

Adjusting fulcrum bridge height

The adjustment process for double-posted fulcrum vibrato systems is identical to the above procedures.

FENDER STYLE BRIDGES

On bridges with individual string height adjustment capabilities, use the following procedure:

1. Raise or lower all strings so they are just above the fret board and ring clearly when plucked.

2. Tune to pitch.

3. Raise or lower each saddle until each string rings clearly with no fret buzz or choke during bends or fretting.

4. Recheck each string at pitch several times and make the minute adjustments necessary to achieve acceptable action on each string.

5. Individual saddles should be of identical adjustment on each side so as not to sit angled or curved in any fashion. This arrangement provides stability and maximum vibrational transfer.

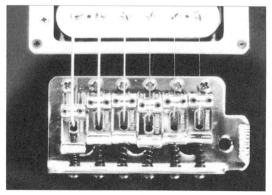

Fender style bridge

6. On bridges with one saddle for every two strings, some concessions to the above (#5) procedure obviously will have to be made. Various and differing saddle adjustments are unavoidable.

GIBSON STYLE COMPENSATING TYPE BRIDGES

On some older instruments and some newer retro-style guitars, you will find a bridge that is a combination of a bridge and a tailpiece. Again, action height is determined by the adjustment of the large slotted screws on each side of the bridge.

ACOUSTIC GUITARS

Most acoustic guitars have a bridge and saddle combination that is fixed, immobile, and incapable of mechanical manipulation. However, some adjustment in height is possible using the following guidelines:

1. Most acoustic guitars, including modern, well-built instruments, have unacceptably high action across the fretboard, especially in the upper positions (even after a truss rod adjustment and a quality set of strings have been installed.) Therefore, the saddle must be reduced in height to lower the action. To accomplish this, you will need to loosen the strings and remove the bridge saddle.

2. To do this, pull the saddle straight up with a pair of pliers. Pull gently, and the saddle should slip from the bridge.

3. Once the saddle is out of the bridge, you must remove some material from its base. Eighty grit sandpaper or a coarse, flat, mill file usually will do the trick. Make sure the base of the saddle is filed level, evenly, and smoothly, so it seats properly when reinstalled in the bridge.

4. Remove only a small amount of material at a time.

5. Reinstall the saddle into the bridge and tune the strings to pitch in order to check the action height.

6. Repeat this procedure until you are satisfied.

In the rare case of the action being too *low,* a new saddle must be constructed. This is a difficult procedure, and requires a high degree of skill. In this case, seek the advice of a professional. If you find grooves in the saddle caused by the strings, the grooves should be gently smoothed away with a file, sandpaper, or synthetic steel wool. If the procedures for action adjustments on acoustics seem beyond your abilities, refer your setup to a competent luthier.

CHAPTER 7

INTONATION ADJUSTMENTS

O nce you are done with your action adjustments, you are ready to intonate the instrument. *Intonation* is the ability of the instrument to play in tune with itself along the entire length of its scale. Intonation also is known as string length compensation. Even though an instrument may be tuned to pitch, it will still play out of tune if not intonated properly. That is, you may tune your instrument's open strings precisely to pitch with the most accurate tuner in the world, yet when you play up and down the neck, some of the notes may be sharp or flat. Chords will sound out of tune. Accurate intonation puts all the notes in tune along the entire length of each string.

TO SET THE INTONATION, FOLLOW THESE STEPS:

1. Tune each string *precisely* to pitch. Small variances will magnify themselves into larger discrepancies when setting intonation.

2. Play the twelfth fret harmonic of the string. This pitch will be one octave higher than the pitch of the open string.

3. Fret the string at the twelfth fret, applying the normal amount of finger pressure you would use during playing. Too little, and the string will buzz, too much and the note will be sharp. Optimally, the twelfth fret harmonic and the twelfth fret fretted note should be exactly the same pitch (and the open string exactly one octave lower). If there is a variance, string length compensation must be performed to put the pitches in unison.

Playing the 12th fret harmonic

4. To make intonation changes, adjustment is simple. If the fretted note is sharp (too high) in relation to the harmonic,

move the saddle backwards towards the bridge and away from the neck. If the fretted note is flat (too low) in relation to the harmonic, move the saddle forward, away from the bridge and towards the neck.

Making an intonation adjustment

5. Remember to re-tune the string to pitch each time you make an adjustment. You may need to do this several times before each string is intonated accurately.

Most guitar and bass intonation adjustments are simple and straightforward; you merely move the saddle in the appropriate direction. However, locking vibrato systems such as Floyd Rose styles use slightly different procedures. Double-locking systems which lock the string at the peg head and saddle are a bit more complicated to intonate. They cause different types of problems and require some patience to adjust, compared to non-locking systems. Here is the basic procedure:

TO ADJUST INTONATION ON A FLOYD ROSE TYPE VIBRATO SYSTEM

1. Loosen string tension on the desired string.

2. Unlock the saddle locking screw.

3. Move the saddle in the appropriate direction.

4. Hold the saddle in place and tighten the saddle locking screw.

5. Tune string back to pitch and recheck intonation.

6. Repeat the above five steps for each string until the instrument is intonated.

You may have to practice a few times as intonating a double locking system takes a little more work and time than standard bridge systems.

CHAPTER 8

PICKUP ADJUSTMENTS

Proper pickup adjustment is essential to proper tonality. Pickups are both the "ears" and "mouth" of the guitar. They "hear" the strings and "speak" to the amplifier. The better a pickup can hear the strings, the better it is able to talk to the amplifier. Although an electric guitar is fundamentally an acoustic instrument, its "electric" voice is dependent upon the pickups. Therefore, proper adjustments will yield noticeable improvements in gain, sustain, noise reduction, and tonality.

In this chapter, I'll show you how to maximize the performance of your pickups. Proper adjustments are the icing on the cake, and help highlight and detail the work you have done on the setup. I'll show you what I have found to be effective and how to get a bigger sound out of your guitar's pickups.

Pickup adjustment is generally the final procedure in a setup. This is also one of the most subjective areas of repair. Players and technicians alike have widely varying opinions on the procedure.

I have had great success setting pickups close to the strings. Doing this allows the pickups to better sense subtleties, and picking dynamics have a broader range. However, you should try variations as you might find adjustments more suited to your taste.

THE FOLLOWING ARE BASIC STEPS TO ADJUSTING PICKUPS:

1. Begin by seating all adjustable pole pieces flush with the surface of the pickup. Then raise the pickup to the strings.

Adjust pickup height

2. Press each string down on the last fret of the fingerboard, insuring the strings clear the pickups. There should be sufficient string clearance so the strings do not touch the pickup during bending or fretted note playing.

3. The pole pieces can then be adjusted individually to each string.

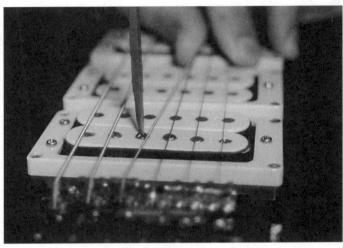

Adjusting polepiece height

My belief is that pickups should be relatively close to the strings. This allows the pickups to hear nuances and subtleties that may be lost if they were lower. This can also make the instrument louder, as the pickup can hear more attack and volume due to the string's close proximity.

Pole piece adjustment can then be done to fine tune the string's relationship to the pickup's magnetic field. You will generally find the pole pieces will resemble the arc of the strings across the fretboard. The pole pieces in the middle will need to be higher as the distance between the strings and the pickup is greater at this point.

CHAPTER 9

ADJUSTING VIBRATO BRIDGES

A djusting guitars equipped with vibrato systems requires patience and precision. Unlike fixed bridge systems, in which you merely install the strings, vibrato bridges maintain an intricate balance between string and spring tension. There are a multitude of different vibrato system designs. I will concentrate on the two most common systems. The traditional types most often found on Fender Stratocaster style guitars, and those of the double-locking, Floyd Rose fulcrum style.

TRADITIONAL STYLE VIBRATO SYSTEMS

To adjust a traditional style vibrato system follow this procedure:

1. Generally at standard pitch (A = 440Hz), only three springs are required for most systems to function correctly, (only two are necessary for .009 gauge string sets). The springs should be well seated on the claw and in the block. They should be arranged with one spring in the middle and one on each side, each parallel with the others.

Vibrato springs

2. Restring the guitar and tune to pitch.

3. Spring tension is controlled by adjusting the claw. To increase tension, screw the spring claw toward the neck. To decrease tension, unscrew the spring claw moving it toward the block. When finished with the tension adjustments the spring claw should remain parallel to the heel of the neck.

Claw adjustment

4. Observe the angle of the bridge base plate in relation to the top of the guitar.

5. The base plate should be tilted slightly forward a few degrees when the guitar is tuned to pitch. The base plate should not be resting on the body. Fender factory specifications state there should be one-half of one step of positive pitch travel available from the bridge using the high E string as a reference pitch. In other words, when you pull up on the vibrato bar, the open E string should come to rest on the pitch F, when the bar is in the full up position. Do not trust your ear on this adjustment. Use an electronic tuner to make an accurate measurement.

Bridge tilt—fulcrum style

6. If there is a lack of positive pitch travel, (less than one-half step) the spring claw must be slightly loosened to allow a greater range of bridge travel.

7. If there is too much of positive pitch travel, (greater than one-half step) the spring claw will have to be tightened to reduce the travel range of the bridge.

The mounting screws that attach the base plate of the bridge to the body at the forward edge of the plate should be screwed into the body as far as possible while still allowing the base plate maximum range of motion. The maximum range of motion is defined as the amount of travel available to the bridge from the resting position of the bridge to the point where the vibrato arm tip touches the body. If the mounting screws are too far into the body, binding will occur between the base plate and the screw tops or pickguard,, thereby limiting travel range. If the screws are too far out of the body, the base plate will jump, shimmy, and/or wobble, becoming unstable and difficult to keep in tune, or operate smoothly. Also, if the screws are too high in relation to the base plate, the shearing forces applied to the screws from the base plate will increase dramatically, which may result in bent or broken screws. Therefore, only unscrew the mounting screws as far as necessary to allow for maximum bridge travel in both directions.

You must continue to make adjustments between spring and string tension until the one half step of upward travel is achieved. This means you must re-tune the strings after every adjustment to maintain accuracy and effectiveness. If you have never done this before, have patience, it takes practice.

The vibrato bar should be screwed into the vibrato block as far as possible without being forced. If you like the bar to swing freely, back off one turn on the threads. A dab of 3-in-1 oil on the threads of the vibrato bar will prevent binding or friction.

FLOATING, FULCRUM STYLE VIBRATO SYSTEMS

1. In most respects the adjustments for a floating system are nearly identical to those of a traditional assembly. However, there is a significant difference in the angle of the base plate in relation to the top of the guitar body. In this case the base plate sits at a right angle to the fulcrum post causing the base plate to rest parallel with the top plane of the body. Also, with these systems there is no specified or particular range of positive pitch travel. The range of upward travel for these systems varies greatly.

2. For spring adjustment of a floating system, follow the aforementioned procedures for traditional vibrato system adjustment. However, in this case you must adjust the base plate to sit level (parallel) in relation to the top of the body instead of angled as with a traditional system.

Bridge tilt—fulcrum style

3. Many fulcrum vibrato systems lock the strings at the head-stock by means of a locking clamp or nut. The nut should be clamped down gently but securely after all other adjustments have been made.

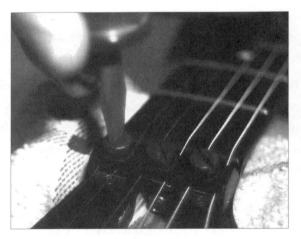

Tightening string clamp

CHAPTER 10

FINAL PROCEDURES AND LONG TERM MAINTENANCE

Finished work

O nce you have completed the set-up procedures in the preceding chapters it is time to help the instrument settle in to its new adjustments. To do this, just play. At this point you are exercising the instrument. I suggest a variety of chord and scale patterns along the neck in all positions using a variety of techniques including bending, to stretch things out.

Enjoy your new set-up!

As you play, be aware how the instrument feels and sounds. Compare it to the original diagnosis you made at the beginning of the setup. Most likely you will find micro adjustments—such as tuning, action, intonation, and possibly even the truss rod—will need to be performed as the instrument stabilizes. This is normal, and unless you change string gauge or brand, very little adjustment will be necessary in the near future.

To keep your instrument playing consistently well, you need only to keep it clean and strung with fresh, quality strings. You will need to check the adjustments periodically to compensate for wear, transport, climatic, and humidity changes. A properly maintained instrument will play well, sound good, and wear well, delivering many years of service before any major repairs (usually to the nut and frets) are required. Until then, rock on!

SELECTED
BIBLIOGRAPHY

Brosh, John, Ed. (nd). *Guitar Gear*. New York, New York: Quill.

Fillet, Peter J. (1984). *D.I.Y. Guitar Repair*. New York, New York: Amsco Publications.

Gibson USA Owner's Manual. (1988). Nashville, Tennessee: Gibson Guitar Corporation.

How to Buy an Electric Guitar. (nd). Nashville, Tennessee: Gibson Guitar Corporation.

Kamimoto, Hideo. (1978). *Complete Guitar Repair*. New York, New York: Oak Publications.

The American Series. (nd). Brea, California: Fender Musical Instruments.